Including Children with Autistic Spectrum Disorders in the Early Years Foundation Stage

Written by
Clare Beswick

Illustrated by
Martha Hardy

Published 2010 by A&C Black Publishers Limited
36 Soho Square, London W1D 3QY
www.acblack.com

ISBN 978-1-4081-294-94

First published in the UK, 2004 Updated 2007
Text © Clare Beswick, 2004
Illustrations © Martha Hardy, 2004

A CIP record for this publication is available from the British Library.
All rights reserved. No part of this publication may be reproduced
in any form or by any means - graphic, electronic, or mechanical, including
photocopying, recording, taping or information storage or retrieval systems -
without the prior permission in writing of the publishers.

Printed in Great Britain by Latimer Trend & Company Limited

This book is produced using paper that is made from wood grown in
managed, sustainable forests. It is natural, renewable and recyclable.
The logging and manufacturing processes conform to the environmental
regulations of the country of origin.

**To see our full range of titles
visit www.acblack.com**

Contents

Introduction	**4**
Key facts about Autism	**6**
What is Autistic Spectrum Disorder (ASD)?	6
Dispelling myths - what you need to know	7
Understanding the triad of impairment	8
Play and autism	10
Making the best of starts	13
The other side of the fence	14
Autistic spectrum disorders and the six areas of the EYFS	**15**
Personal, social and emotional development	15
Communication, language and literacy	15
Problem solving, reasoning and numeracy	15
Knowledge and understanding of the world	16
Physical development	16
Creative development	16
Developing Key Skills	**17**
Gaining attention and developing shared attention	17
Taking turns	18
Using and developing pointing	20
Building anticipation -'Are you ready?'	22
Using simple pretend play	23
Using music	25
Using balls, hoops and other small apparatus	27
Running, chasing and bouncing	28
Using water play	30
Using computers, television and DVDs	31
Using creative activities	33
Using photos, pictures and books	34
Differentiation and reinforcement	**37**
Who's who in multi-agency working?	**40**
Partnership with parents	**41**
Different approaches to helping children with Autistic Spectrum Disorders	**43**
Resources and websites	**46**
Key contacts	**47**

Introduction

The Early Years Foundation Stage is an exciting time for young children. It enables children to be active learners, to be partners in play, to imagine, create, discover and explore. The freedom and flexibility of provision in the EYFS makes very real demands for many children with autistic spectrum disorders, presenting unique challenges for the child and early years practitioners. With energy, determination and imagination, inclusion of children with autism in the Early Years Foundation Stage can work.

This book will help you make the most of the Early Years Foundation Stage for young children with autistic spectrum disorders. It aims to inform, encourage and reassure you. Early years practitioners are experts in early childhood and have a unique opportunity to really get to know and tune into individual children. The skills, experience and insight you have gained as an early years practitioner are essential ingredients in making inclusion really work for all children in your setting.

This book will:

Inform you by:

- providing essential background information, dispel myths and provide key facts
- signposting you to further resources
- telling you about the implications of autistic spectrum disorders for learning across the areas of learning in the EYFS
- defining who's who in the multi agency team
- guiding you through some different approaches or ways of working.

Support you by:

- giving tried and tested teaching tips
- helping you to plan the environment and organisation
- suggesting ideas and activities using everyday resources
- helping you to be an essential part of a multi agency team
- offering practical ideas for differentiation.

Inspire you by:
- giving insight into the parents' perspective
- suggesting loads of easy activity ideas
- describing good ideas for a smooth start to learning in your setting.

Make you think by asking:
- how might it feel to have an autistic spectrum disorder?
- what's it like to feel different?
- what is it like to parent a child with special needs?
- how can you help other children understand autism?

Make you ask yourself some hard questions such as:
- how can I make real connections with this child?
- what do I need to do for this child to enable them to make the most of the Early Years Foundation Stage?
- how can I help children understand, value and support others in my setting?

Who is this book for?

This book is for anyone with an interest in very young children with autistic spectrum disorders, students and early years practitioners. Many of the practical ideas and suggestions are suitable for children with developmental delay, and can be easily adapted for children of different ages who have communication difficulties, and are working at this developmental stage.

The activity pages:

All the activity pages are:
- packed with easy to do ideas, using everyday resources
- planned specifically for children with autistic spectrum disorders
- linked to the early learning goals in the Early Years Foundation Stage Framework
- contain lots of opportunities for small step learning, repetition and reinforcement
- written to take careful account of the implications of autistic spectrum disorders on individual children's learning.

Key facts about Autism

What is Autism (ASD)?

Autism is a lifelong developmental disorder, present from birth, that affects the way a child relates to and understands others. It is a complex disorder and every individual is affected differently. Many children with autism also have additional learning difficulties.

Each individual may have a mild to severe degree of autism, and may have anything from severe learning difficulties to a high level of intelligence. This continuum of degree of autism and also learning ability is known as the autistic continuum. Individuals can be anywhere on the autistic continuum and be described as having an autistic spectrum disorder.

Some children who are of average or above average intelligence, and less severely autistic may be described as having Asperger's syndrome.

Every child with autistic spectrum disorder is unique and may be very different from others in terms of their abilities, interests and challenges. However they all have difficulties in the following three areas:

- Communication
- Social interaction
- Rigidity of thinking, problems with imagination and creativity.

This is known as the triad of impairment.

Getting a diagnosis

Although autism is present from birth many children are not diagnosed with an autistic spectrum disorder until they are at least two and half years old, and in many cases, much older. Therefore, it is likely that there will be children starting in the Foundation Stage where parents and or practitioners have concerns about the child's development, but problems have not yet been diagnosed, and others who may be being currently assessed or have very recently had a diagnosis.

If you have concerns about a child's development, it is important to discuss this supportively with the parents and advise them to approach their family doctor, or health visitor. Also discuss your concerns with the special needs co-ordinator and senior member of staff.

Dispelling the myths – what you need to know

- Autism is a lifelong developmental disorder.
- It is present from birth but may not be recognised until much later.
- There is no cure, but there is much that can be done to help.
- It is four times more common in boys than girls.
- Many of the children also have learning difficulties.
- It affects each child differently but all have difficulties with communication, social interaction and rigidity of thinking.
- The cause of autism is unknown, but research suggests there may be a number of triggers.
- A few individuals with autism have special or 'savant' skills, perhaps a remarkable memory for or obsession with numbers, or ability to draw extremely accurate pictures of complex scenes, but this is the exception rather than the norm.
- Some children have obsessional behaviours, such as spinning, tapping, lining objects up or other obsessive and often repeated activities.
- Others have special interests that they pursue to the exclusion of other activities, such as trains, for example Thomas the Tank Engine; or perhaps telephone numbers.
- Several approaches are used to help children with autism, (see page 43), but all address the triad of impairment.

And particular issues for the early years:

Early intervention is very important:

- All young children with autism have difficulty with communication skills. They may be pre-verbal or use lots of words or sentences but they will have difficulties in the way they use language to communicate.
- Some children may be over sensitive to certain stimuli, such as loud noises, bright lights, moving objects such as escalators or lifts, or have extreme food fads.
- Helping very young children make sense of the world and develop early communication skills needs you to have knowledge, insight, flexibility, determination and support.
- Intervention must focus on the three key areas of the triad of impairment – communication, social interaction and rigidity of thinking.

Understanding the effect of the triad of impairment

All children with autistic spectrum disorders, with or without additional learning difficulties have a degree of difficulty in the each part of the triad of impairment.

- Communication
- Social Interaction
- Rigidity of thinking, impaired imagination or creativity, or obsessive or rigid behaviours.

The degree of difficulty and how this affects each child will vary according to the child's ability to learn, individual circumstances and experiences, the environment, and the way those around them interact with them.

Communication
Many young children with autism will have difficulty with all aspects of communication: Eye contact; understanding and using gesture and facial expressions; body language; pointing; as well as with understanding and using spoken language. Some young children with autism, particularly those with Asperger's syndrome, may appear to understand and use spoken language but may have difficulties in the way they use language to communicate. They may be very literal in their understanding and expression, may have difficulties with the social timing of conversation, or picking up the non-verbal messages from others that are essential to effective communication.

Social Interaction
Again each child will be affected differently. Some children may appear withdrawn and to prefer to be alone, others may appear odd or aloof, others may have difficulty with empathy or being aware that others may have a different view of the world to their own.

Rigidity of thinking or behaviour
Some children may have obsessive behaviours, such as lining up objects, spinning or flapping their hands or a bit of ribbon, others may have an obsessive need for routine, such as always drinking from the same cup, or always following the same route between places. Some may be very literal in their thinking, be rigid, unable to be imaginative or creative and have great difficulty developing simple pretend play.

The world as a confusing place

For a very young child with autism the world is a confusing place. The way they seem to perceive the world is different from other children. As well as having difficulty in understanding, communicating and interacting with others, the child may indeed physically perceive the world in a different way. Information received by the senses may be interpreted differently, perhaps making the child fascinated by light being filtered through leaves on a tree, upset by certain noises, such as vacuum cleaners or startled by sudden loud noises, such as a balloon popping.

Routine and order help to make the world easier to interpret and find their way around. Structure and consistency can make the world and the way we respond more predictable, safer and more understandable to the child with an autistic spectrum disorder.

Making a difference

The early years setting is potentially a very confusing place for children with autism, but there is much that can be done, simply and inexpensively to make the environment less daunting. Exactly what needs to be done, will depend on the individual child's needs, but consider some of the following strategies:

- Take photographs of key events such as story time, milk time and so on. Make a visual diary or timetable and use these cards to help the child know what is happening next.

- Use real reminders, such as a cushion or mat to define the space the child should sit in at story time.

- Try to create a calm space, for gentle interactive play.

- Make a small work area for structured one to one learning, preferably at a small table, with space for the practitioner to sit opposite the child.

- Remove distractions from the work area.

- Collect real everyday objects for teaching simple pretend play and imitating the use of objects.

Play and autism

Children with autism need help to make sense of the world and encouragement and support to develop communication and interaction skills. In the early years settings, practitioners can:

- play alongside, modelling play and encouraging communication and interaction

- focus on interactive play to engage the child, develop a shared attention and work on early communication and social interaction skills, such as anticipation, pointing and turn taking

- provide short bursts of structured learning, using a step by step approach to teach new skills, and develop communication skills, from reaching or pointing to understanding of single words, to far more complex language tasks, such as making requests, asking questions, or understanding concepts such as big and little

- follow the child's lead, imitating sounds and movement, or providing a simple singing commentary.

Indeed, in many settings, practitioners will need to use all these strategies at different times, in response to the needs of the child. In addition to these strategies, the early years practitioner needs to:

- focus on communication and social interaction
- seize the moment when the child is ready and relaxed
- build predictable sequences
- use routines consistently
- plan real rewards for the child
- reduce the amount of language, using simple short phrases
- use the child's name first, such as '*name* look'
- teach touch and distance pointing
- respect the child's view of the world.

Play is the work of the child in the early years. It is critical to all learning in the Foundation Stage and is very difficult for many young children with autistic spectrum.

Why is play so difficult for children with autistic spectrum disorders?

Play and social development go hand in hand. Social interaction is an integral part of almost all play. If you think of the earliest play of tiny babies it is people play, as they recognise faces and interact with their parents. This interactive play enables babies and toddlers to find out about their world, explore and discover everyday objects, what the objects do and how they can have an effect on objects and people in their world.

Among many other opportunities, play helps young children to:

- find out about their world and their place in it
- test out ideas, make discoveries
- explore their feelings and fears
- be imaginative and creative
- learn about co-operation, sharing and working together, being part of a group
- work out how people behave in different situations
- develop symbolic understanding, where one object represents another.

The play of many children with autism is often:

- repetitive
- comforting to the child rather than explorative or developmental
- stimulating and rewarding to the individual but often difficult for others to understand
- an attempt to make sense of a confusing world.

Play is the work of the child in the early years. It is critical to all learning in the Foundation Stage and is very difficult for many young children with autistic spectrum.

Using interactive play

Interactive play can be used to develop communication and social interaction skills, and particularly to engage the child with autism who may appear aloof, or 'in their own world'. It can be used to gain the attention of children and build shared attention when you are both focused on the same object or activity but are also each aware that the other is involved. It is about sharing the emotions and the actions as well as the same physical space. Shared attention is fundamental to developing a need or intention or desire to communicate.

You can use interactive play to develop:

- shared attention
- anticipation
- turn taking
- pointing
- imitating sounds, and so on.

During sessions of interactive play, practitioners need to:

- follow the child's lead
- use hesitation and pauses to help the child know that they need to make a sound or action
- use familiar songs and routines, such as tickle games to build sequences that gain the child's attention and encourage communication.

For other children, interactive play can be used to:

- encourage expressive language
- help the child make requests, ask questions
- learn about words to describe feelings, such as happy, sad, tired, hungry, thirsty.

For the young child with an autistic spectrum disorder the essential ingredients of communication and social interaction are impaired, making interactive play difficult.

Using structured play

Structured play offers the opportunity for children with autism to work step by step towards gaining new skills in a predictable sequence. Although this does little to encourage creativity and natural discovery, it does help the child to gain valuable skills and develop their understanding. It can also be used to teach communication, such as pointing or recognising pictures. Structured play breaks down activities into chunks, so that it is no longer a jumble of words, actions and objects. This breaking down of an activity into its component parts helps the young child with autism, work out the meaning of each part.

Early years practitioners are accustomed to breaking down tasks into small achievable steps for younger children just starting out in the Foundation Stage. Providing this very structured activity can be a very natural process for them.

Structured play will also help the child to:

- have a clear objective
- involve predictable consistent sequences
- be part of a fixed routine
- have minimum distractions
- build on the child's strengths as well as addressing difficulties
- include a routine for getting started and a clear signal that it is ended, such as sitting opposite the child and singing 'hello' to them to get started, and perhaps putting all the toys in a box and putting a lid on it, and saying 'finished' at the end.

Finally, and importantly …

Structured play may seem to be at odds with the philosophy of the Early Years Foundation Stage and a play-based curriculum, but children with autism do not generally have a motivation to interact, talk and play with other children and do not learn through natural discovery. The purpose of their play and activity is often to maintain sameness and repetition. So structured play can be an important element in the range of opportunities provided for the child with an autistic spectrum disorder in the Foundation Stage.

Making the best of starts

Change is especially hard for children with autism and starting nursery is likely to be a particular anxious time for parents, so make time to prepare for the best of starts for the child, parents and everyone in your setting.

- Every child is different. Take time to observe the child at home as well as in other settings, such as parent and toddler group.

- Visit the parents at home and listen to their concerns and hopes for their child at school.

- Find out how their child lets them know what they want, perhaps by looking, reaching, words. Do they use any gestures or symbols to help their child's understanding?

- Find out about favourite activities and toys. Ask about special interests.

- Talk about self-help skills and plan how you will help the child to become independent, and learn nursery routines.

- Ask about other professional involvement and request names and contact numbers if this seems appropriate. Find out what they are working on and if possible observe them at work with the child.

- Get involved in the multi agency team providing support to the family, so that you can plan together to help the child get the most from the Early Years Foundation Stage.

- Explain the role of the key person and plan how the team can work together.

- Be clear with the parents what is to be provided for their child and how you will plan and ensure their child's needs are met. Make sure they have the chance to meet the special needs co-ordinator and find out about their role and responsibilities.

- Make sure the parents realise that you are learning about autistic spectrum disorders, but are really keen to get to know their child as an individual.

- Make sure all the staff understand a little about autism and the triad of impairment.

- Explain your goals and plan how you are going to work together as a team to support the child.

The other side of the fence

Finding out that your child has an autistic spectrum disorder throws most parents onto a roller coaster of conflicting and changing emotions. Parents of young children with an autistic spectrum disorder in the Foundation Stage are likely to still be on this roller coaster and need particular support.

Working together to meet the needs of their child will give parents:

confidence and hope
greater insight
knowledge, tips and ideas.

It will also allow them to:

share the anxiety
enjoy their child.

Early years practitioners have the skills and experience to work effectively with all parents, and particularly parents under stress. Having learnt a little about this most complex of disorders and begun to see how autism is expressed in a particular child, further insight can be gained by trying to imagine how the world might seem to that child. You can do this by listening to parents and really watching their child, trying to tune into their interactions and communications, and thinking about how they respond to different situations and people.

Personal accounts written by older children and adults with autism and Asperger's syndrome give a unique insight into how the world might seem to the child with autism. Although each account is very personal and highly individual, common themes do emerge as adults reflect on their early childhood experiences. There are many personal accounts and you can find links to further resources through the website of the National Autistic Society. For full contact details of these and other organisations, see page 47.

It is likely that the very young child with an autistic spectrum disorder experiences intense feelings of anxiety, confusion and frustration, so the repetitive behaviours that you may observe in some children with autism could be viewed as a perfectly ordinary reaction to coping with intense stress and confusion brought on by a constantly changing, unfathomable world.

Autistic spectrum disorders and the six areas of the EYFS

Young children with autistic spectrum disorders will have more difficulty in some areas of learning than others, although their difficulties with communication and social interaction are likely to pervade the way they learn across all areas of learning.

Personal, social and emotional development

Personal, social and emotional development with its emphasis on relationships, and understanding the needs of others, presents unique challenges to the child with autism, although there is much that can be done to help children develop early social interaction skills, and to help more able children develop sharing, turn taking, and strategies to work towards developing understanding of others and towards establishing friendships.

Communication, language and literacy

Communication, language and literacy are likely to be particularly challenging, with most children needing an individual plan to develop their earliest communication skills to work towards the first stepping stones. Establishing an effective means of communication is very important and should be a part of everything the child does in the early years. Some children may be pre-verbal, needing work to develop eye contact, turn taking, babble sounds as well as pointing and simple gestures. Other children may use long strings of words and here the aim will be to build the communicative intent and purposes for which communication is used.

Problem solving, reasoning and numeracy

With a structured step-by-step approach, children with autism may work effectively towards goals in Problem Solving, Reasoning and Numeracy. Good memory skills, and the concrete and predictable nature of early mathematical concepts may help the more able child with autism do well in this area of learning.

Knowledge and understanding of the world

Routine, structure and sensory exploration will help the child with autism begin to gain knowledge and understanding of the world and how they might operate in it. Real life opportunities with everyday objects and following established routines will help the child to find out about the world, starting with the real, everyday events that are most significant to the individual child.

Physical Development

Every child is different, but many young children with autism enjoy active lively physical play. In physical development children with autistic spectrum disorders need to be encouraged to work alongside others and as part of a group. Lively active play can be a great way to teach and reward children's communication and social interaction skills.

Creative Development

Creative development will be particularly complicated because children with autistic spectrum disorders have difficulty with imagination, and rigidity of thought and behaviour. Children need to be taught simple pretend play and to be encouraged to experiment with different sounds, music and sensory play.

The wealth of activities and experiences provided in the Early Years Foundation Stage offer the chance for practitioners to:

- recognise the most rewarding experiences for the child and use these to motivate and focus learning
- teach key skills in the areas of communication and social interaction using a flexible range of exciting resources
- meet individual needs while the child is alongside others.

Early years settings however offer unique challenges to the child with autism, as they are often busy, bright, stimulating, noisy, challenging places, but their flexibility allows the practitioner to find ways of organising the learning environment and allows for flexible rewards to be offered to the child. It also allows the practitioner to work in close partnership with the parents and other professionals involved. This should ensure a consistent approach and shared objectives.

Developing Key Skills

Gaining attention and developing shared attention

Why is this skill important?

- Some young children with autism prefer to be solitary or aloof, avoiding shared attention. They may be distressed by attempts to gain eye contact, physical contact or to interact with others, on the other person's terms. Observe carefully, go slowly and try to tune in to the needs of the individual child.

- You need to start by gaining the child's attention, then move into shared attention, where you are both focused on the same activity and are each aware that the other is involved. Both parties' attention is essential to the activity.

- Shared attention is essential to help the child interact, develop communication skills and be able to focus on a task in a more structured activity. Persevere in helping them to develop this vital skill!

- Watch for the things they enjoy. Remember that interactive play aimed at developing attention and shared attention should be fun for both of you.

Attention and the EYFS Guidance

Children will probably be working at an early developmental stage such as:

- PSED: feel safe and secure and show a sense of trust; seek out others to share experiences; relate and make attachments to members of their group; build relationships with special people

- CLL: communicate in a variety of ways including crying, gurgling, babbling and squealing; use single word and two word utterances to convey simple and more complex messages

- PD: move spontaneously within the available space; respond to rhythm, music and story by means of gesture and movement

Ideas and activities to try

- Try some gentle tickle play. Call the child's name and then go to tickle him, pausing before tickling him. Tickle for a moment, then stop and see if the child makes any sort of movement, gesture or glance to suggest he wants you to do it again. Ask, 'again?' pause and wait for a glance, or even a stilling of his movement.
Take this as a 'yes' and say, '*name*, yes, more' and tickle again.

- Try this sequence while bouncing a balloon on the child's knees or hands.
- Join in with the child's play, so if they are stamping or patting, copy their actions. If they change actions, change yours to be the same. Pause for a moment, and see if they do another action for you to copy. Are they aware that you are imitating them?
- Play at making funny faces and sounds. Encourage the child to touch your nose. As they touch your nose, make a funny noise. Try it again. Make the same sound each time he touches your nose. Gently touch his nose and make a different sound.
- Play peek-a-boo, pausing after each repetition to give the child a chance to use eye contact, facial expression or body language to say 'again'.
- Jogging on knee rhymes are great fun, and bring a sense of shared fun to many children.
- Try dancing together, rocking and swaying hand in hand to music. Stop and wait for the child to look at you, or in another way let you know that s/he wants you to continue.

Tips for teaching

- Seize the right moment! Observe the child carefully to see when they are most open to communication, when they are most relaxed.
- Imitating a child's actions can be a really good way to gain their attention.
- If sitting face to face is too much for the child, start playing side-by-side or even with the child facing away from you. Work towards getting them face to face with you as soon as they are ready.
- Make pauses between activities very definite and obvious.
- Making an exaggerated gasp can be a great way to gain a child's attention.
- Try this sort of interactive play with gentle rough and tumble games, or chasing games outside.

Taking turns

Why is this skill important?

- Taking turns is an important part of everyday life and essential for developing effective communication and learning to be part of a group.
- Taking turns is a very important part of early communication and interaction. In its simplest form, it is about physically taking turns to do the same action. It grows into imitating and taking turns with sounds, actions and even words.

- Turn taking is an important part of the 'to and fro' of conversation. To take turns you need to be aware of the other person and be ready to interact with them. Some children with autistic spectrum disorders need to be taught turn taking.

- For pre-verbal children working on earliest communication skills, turn taking is about imitation, and physical turn taking. For other children it is about taking turns with sounds, reciprocal babble, or perhaps learning to take turns to talk and listen, in the two-way process of communication.

Turn taking and the EYFS Guidance

Children will probably be working at an early developmental stage such as:

- PSED: enjoy the company of others; seek out others to share experiences; depend on close attachments with a special person within their setting; learn by interacting with others

- CLL: use talk to gain attention and sometimes use action rather than talk to demonstrate or explain to others

Ideas and activities to try

- Try banging a drum or tambourine. Start by imitating the child's actions and then gradually try to get a turn taking sequence established. Try this with chime bars, tambours and other instruments. Begin with turn taking using just one instrument, and progress to an instrument each.

- Try turn taking simple physical actions, such as stamping feet, clapping hands and so on. Start by imitating the child's actions.

- Take turns to add bricks to a tower, pegs in a tin, shapes in a posting box.

- Try to introduce some simple pretend play, perhaps taking turns to wipe a doll's face with a flannel, put on a hat, pass a cup of tea.

- Take turns to pour a jug of water or sand. Say 'gone' and pause before saying '*name's* turn'.

- Listen for and copy sounds that the child makes. Try to develop a turn taking sequence with simple sounds, as you would when babbling with a young baby.

- If children are ready for more, try turn taking with simple lotto cards, taking turns to match a picture, taking turns to whizz cars down a ramp, or perhaps to paint a stripe on paper or make a mark with chalk.

Tips for teaching

- Use special interests to help gain and maintain attention on turn taking activities. The child who loves trains may enjoy taking turns to add another coach to a train, one who loves lining up objects may enjoy adding another brick to a line, or a cube to a stack.

- Plan opportunities for turn taking play for each play area, such as turn taking with marks at the mark making table, taking turns in the sand tray, taking turns to prod the dough/use a cutter at the dough table, and so on.

- Look for quiet turn taking opportunities as well as more active ones, such as taking turns to press the space bar on the computer or turning the pages in a book.

- Use a touch pointing gesture to remind children when it is their turn; point and touch the object, 'look, *name's* turn'.

Using and developing pointing

Why is this skill important?

- Many babies start to use a pointing gesture around the time they are eleven months old.

- Most children with autistic spectrum disorders find using a pointing gesture difficult, but it can be a very effective communicative tool once it has developed.

- There are different kinds of pointing:
  - pointing to make a request, such as 'I want', or 'give me' …
  - pointing to share something, perhaps to mean 'look at that', and at the same time looking to the other person to check that they have seen what you are pointing at
  - touch pointing – when you make a pointing gesture while physically touching the object
  - distance pointing – pointing in the direction of an object or event.

- Teaching young children with autistic spectrum disorders to point can be very helpful and needs to start with touch pointing.

- A pointing gesture can be used to make choices, make requests, gain attention, share information and much more, but always needs to be modelled alongside a word or label.

Pointing and the EYFS Guidance

Children will probably be working at an early developmental stage such as:

- CLL: are able to respond to simple requests and grasp meaning from context; respond to words and interactive rhymes

Ideas and activities to try

- Blow some bubbles for the child to pop. This helps the child isolate an index finger to form a pointing gesture. Encourage them to touch point to the bubble pot for more bubbles.

- Practise picking up tiny hundreds and thousands, or sequins using a damp finger and a pointing gesture.

- Do an inset jigsaw puzzle together. Keep all the pieces and offer the child a choice of two. Help them to point to the puzzle piece they want.

- Try this with lotto pictures and a lotto board. The child could point to the picture they want, or perhaps point to show you a matching picture, or if they are ready to point out a named picture, using pointing to either make a choice, match or select a picture.

- Use simple pop up toys. Encourage the child to point to choose which box they want to be opened next.

- Practise sorting two sets of objects, such as toy cars in one box, bricks in another. Help the child to point to the box in which each item should be placed. Try this with everyday objects too, such as sorting spoons and cups, or shoes and socks.

(Tips for teaching)

- Model and use a pointing gesture yourself. Add a pointing gesture to songs and rhymes. Use pointing when showing storybook pictures.

- Encourage the child to use a pointing gesture to make choices, 'Which cup do you want?' Show two and help them to point at the cup they want. Gently take their hand and form their fingers into a pointing gesture, touch point to the object of their choice.

- Play 'Simon Says touch your nose', and so on. Next try a pointing version, such as 'Simon says point to the door' and so on.

- Offer choices between two objects whenever possible.

- Sometimes, put some objects that the child wants out of reach, so that they have to use a pointing gesture to make a request.

- Teach pointing consistently, but to get the best response choose the moment when the child is most receptive, focused and motivated.

- Have realistic expectations and understand that progress may be slow and inconsistent.

Building anticipation - 'Are you ready?'

Why is this skill important?

- Anticipation is an important step in the before words stage of language development. It comes naturally to many children, but some children with autism need to be taught anticipation.

- Anticipating that something is about to happen, or someone else is about to speak is an important early social interaction and communication skill.

- Using 'Ready steady go' anticipation play is a helpful way to gain shared attention and early interaction skills with some children with autistic spectrum disorders.

- You will already be doing lots of anticipation games with the youngest children, such as action rhymes and finger rhymes with an element of anticipation such as 'Round and Round the Garden Like a Teddy Bear', 'Five Fat Peas in a Pea Pod Pressed'.

Anticipation and the EYFS Guidance

Children will probably be working at an early developmental stage such as:

- PSED: look to others for responses which confirm, contribute to, or challenge their understanding of themselves; learn by interacting with others

- CLL: use words and/or gestures, including body language such as eye contact and facial expression to communicate: respond to simple instructions; use isolated words and phrases and/or gesture to communicate with those well known to them; engage in activities requiring hand-eye co-ordination

Ideas and activities to try

- Offer a choice of two balloons. Encourage the child to indicate a choice, using a pointing gesture/and or words. Blow up the balloon they choose, say 'Ready, steady go'. Pause before you say 'go', to give the child a chance to use eye contact, gesture or words to encourage you to let the balloon go. Say 'go' and let the balloon go. Watch together as it whizzes around the room. Play again.

- Try this sequence with simple wind up toys. Focus on pausing before 'go', to build the sense of anticipation, as well as giving the child a clue that some sort of communication is expected from them.

- Play 'Ready, steady go' with a spinning top or simply spinning a hoop. Introduce an element of turn taking, by providing two tops or hoops and encouraging the child to use a touch or distance pointing gesture and/or words to indicate their choice.

- Try blowing clean feathers across the room after saying 'Ready, steady...... go!' This works well with tissue paper squares or a silky scarf.

- Add another element by peering through coloured cellophane or tissue, smiling at the child and playing 'Peek a boo', before playing 'Ready, steady go' and blowing the paper across the room.

- Play 'Ready, steady go' before pushing teddy down the slide. Try this with balls, cars and other wheeled toys.

Tips for teaching

- An element of surprise may be the last thing some children with autism want! They prefer their world to be predictable and organised. Go gently with the surprise, getting to know the individual child well and tuning in to their perception of the world, so you can plan enjoyable and effective activities.

- Introduce 'Ready, steady go' into some gentle rough and tumble play, jumping in puddles together or running and stopping.

- Get together with other early years practitioners and make a list of all the finger rhymes and action rhymes with an element of surprise. Keep this list handy for spare moments.

- Try Jack in the Box type surprise toys.

- Keep the surprise element low key. Keep the child focused on the activity and the anticipation. Make your voice level and tone low and quiet to avoid over excitement.

Using simple pretend play

Why is this skill important?

- Imagination and creativity are of fundamental importance to us all, as adults as well as during childhood. They enable us to work through experiences, fears and imagine how we may feel and respond in different situations. Imaginative play provides children with a safe place to try out and explore new ideas as well as manage stresses and anxieties.

- Imaginative play is particularly difficult for children with autistic spectrum disorders. They tend to be very literal in their thinking and rigid in their play, so there is much to be gained from systematically teaching simple pretend play.

- Simple pretend play with everyday things helps children learn about object use and everyday routines and sequences.

- Imitating actions is an important part of the way in which we learn. Copying everyday tasks and sequences is a good way to start.

Simple pretend play and the EYFS Guidance

Children will probably be working at an early developmental stage such as:

- PSED: develop an understanding and awareness of themselves
- CLL: use talk to gain attention and sometimes use action rather than talk to demonstrate or explain to others
- CD: Notice what adults do, imitating what is observed and then doing it spontaneously when the adult is not there; begin to make believe by pretending

Ideas and activities to try

- Encourage the child to join in simple tasks, such as having a duster each and working together to dust some shelves, or using a pair of damp sponges to wipe down a bike together.
- Break down complex tasks into simple chunks. Play at drying cups that have been washed, rather than working through the whole sequence of clearing up and washing up together. Breaking down the play into component tasks makes the play scenario easier to understand, imitate and with time, develop further.
- Focus on ordinary everyday activities familiar to the child.
- Pretend to give teddy a drink. Encourage the child to copy the actions with their own teddy and cup. Use visual clues, such as a photograph of the cup being held to teddy's mouth.
- Build up sequences of simple pretend play, such as feeding teddy and then washing teddy's face when the child can copy the first part of a sequence.
- Use two matching sets of miniature small world toys. Encourage the child to copy your actions with the toys, or if they play spontaneously with the toys, you copy their actions and provide a simple commentary. Talk about what they are doing. You could try singing the commentary!

Tips for teaching

- Choose simple, familiar props to develop pretend play.
- Small world play with life-like miniatures can be a useful way to work towards imaginative play for children with autistic spectrum disorders.
- Use two sets of toys when teaching a child to copy actions, one for them and one for you.

- Define the space in which you are playing, such as putting a table mat on a table, or a plain rug or tray if you are playing on the floor. Avoid patterned backgrounds as they can add confusion.

- Use simple words to build short repetitive phrases describing what you and the child are doing, such as:

    Brushing baby's hair

    Brushing baby's hair

    Washing baby's face

    Washing baby's face

    Goodnight, baby, goodnight

Using music

Why is this skill important?

- Many children with autism have auditory processing difficulties. This means that some children are hypersensitive to particular sounds. Some children are distressed by unexpected sounds or sounds of a certain pitch.

- Vacuum cleaners, popping balloons and hot air hand dryers, as well as high-pitched buzzers are some examples of the sounds that children with autism may be hypersensitive to.

- Familiar songs and tunes can be a comfort when a child is stressed or upset. They can block out distressing factors.

- Used sensitively, music can be a great way in to early interaction play.

Music and the EYFS Guidance

Children will probably be working at an early developmental stage such as:

- PD: move spontaneously within available space; respond to rhythm, music and story by means of gesture and movement; use movement to express feelings

- CD: show an interest in the way musical instruments sound; respond to sound with body movement; enjoy joining with dancing and ring games; begin to move rhythmically; show an interest in what they see, hear, smell, touch and feel

Ideas and activities to try

- Try dancing together. Let the child stand on your feet as you move together to the music. Pause often, and encourage the child to ask you to start again with a glance, a gesture, body language or words.
- Play rolling or rocking from side to side to the music.
- Try a real or homemade drum and sound out the beat together.
- Sing commentaries to the child describing what they are doing, such as 'Jade is jumping, jumping, jumping, Jade is jumping, jump, jump, jump'.
- Try '*name* do this, do this, do this, *name* do this, just like me', for copying actions.
- Put together a treasure basket of musical instruments or sound makers. Watch the child carefully. See which sounds and rhythms are most appealing. Use these as rewards or motivators, or to soothe and relax the child.
- Play musical bumps with familiar music. Encourage the child to ask for the music to start again, with a point, glance, body language or words.
- Encourage making choices.
- Offer choices of musical instrument or tapes.

Tips for teaching

- Sung commentaries are often more acceptable to the child and feel more natural to the adult. You don't need to be good at singing!
- Try playing music in different settings, such as outside, from a radio, on a CD or tape player, through headphones and so on.
- Experiment with different types of music. Try dance, classical, electronic, pop, jazz, reggae or country-dance music.
- Relax together in the story corner with some soft toys, while playing some soothing music
- Try story tapes. Often words without the demands of social interaction are easier for the child to process or tolerate.

Using balls, hoops and other small apparatus

Why is this skill important?

- Some children with autism have difficulties with balance and coordination; some may be extremely active or hyperactive, others may be less active than you would expect of a young child.

- This is a result of the difficulties many children with autism have with processing sensory information, which may range from a different response to information on taste, smell, touch or vision, or from the vestibular system, related to balance and coordination, certain colours and so on.

- You need to know the child! Talking to parents, listening, observing and tuning into the child's needs and responses will help you to find out how these sensory processing difficulties may be affecting the individual child.

Using small apparatus and the EYFS Guidance

Children will probably be working at an early developmental stage such as:

- PSED: enjoy the company of others; learn by interacting with others

- CLL: use words and or/gestures, including body language, such as eye contact and facial expression to communicate; respond to simple instructions; use actions, sometimes with limited talk, that is largely concerned with the 'here and now'

- PD: move spontaneously within the available space; can stop; move freely with pleasure and confidence; combine and repeat a range of movements; use increasing control over an object by touching, pushing, patting, throwing, catching or kicking it

Ideas and activities to try

- Bounce a ball vigorously up and down in front of you. Catch the ball suddenly and say, 'Stop!' Ask 'Again?'

- Take it in turns to throw beanbags against a wall. 'Splat! Again?'

- Play 'Ready steady ….pause …go' before rolling a ball to the child.

- Spin a hoop. Catch it suddenly and say 'Stop!' Encourage the child to ask for more with a look, gesture, point, or words.

- Lie the child on a beach ball and gently rock them back and forth. Stop and pause for a moment to see if the child will ask for more.

- Roll balls down a slide or through a card tube to the child. Say 'Give me' with an outstretched hand gesture for the child to return the ball for another go.
- Try throwing balls or sponges into a bucket of water for a good attention grabber!
- Practise passing a beanbag back and forth, or round a small group of children.

Tips for teaching

- Using set routines for each game or activity helps the child anticipate what is going to happen next, and what is expected from them.
- Using simple repetitive language, and sung commentaries or simple rhymes will help the child get involved and imitate actions, as well as promoting early understanding of language.
- Rolling and throwing balls back and forth are great for simple turn taking and 'Ready steady go' play.
- Rolled up socks make good substitute balls for really vigorous play without risk of injury or breakages!
- Look out for balls, beanbags and hoops of different textures and colours. Try reflective balls, noisy balls, 'koosh' balls, textured beanbags. Observe which are most appealing to the child and use this information to make other activities equally appealing.

Running, chasing and bouncing

Why is this skill important?

- Processing information from the vestibular system may be difficult for some children with autism, leading to difficulties with balance and coordination. Others may have excellent balance and know no fear!
- Rocking and bouncing is particularly satisfying to some children with autistic spectrum disorders. This can be a good motivator, or if they are too focused on the movement it can get in the way of learning. Observing the child and listening to parents and others involved with them will be the best way to find out how the child might be affected.
- Outdoor play is very important for all children in the Early Years Foundation Stage, but particularly so for children with autism because it gives them the space to run off excess energy and Practice balance and coordination as well as coping with the very different sensory experience of being outside in a safe and controlled way.

Running, chasing, bouncing and the EYFS Guidance

Children will probably be working at an early developmental stage such as:

- PD: move with control and co-ordination; move spontaneously within the available space; can stop; adjust speed or change direction to avoid obstacles; jump off and object and land appropriately; judge body space in relation to spaces available when fitting into confined spaces or negotiating holes and boundaries

Ideas and activities to try

- Chalk a line on the floor and Practise jumping over it, 'Ready, steady …pause…go!'
- Hold long ribbons or scarves and run around with the scarves floating behind. Encourage follow the leader.
- Use a fabric tunnel or large cardboard box and play a game of taking turns to scramble through the box or tunnel.
- Try imitating the child's spontaneous actions, and see if they make new actions for you to copy. Are they aware that you are copying their actions?
- Play chasing a ball, rolling it down a gentle slope or card tube. See if you can catch it before it gets to the bottom.
- Race around with a pull-a long toy. 'Can you catch it?' Pause for body language, gesture, pointing or words to ask for the activity to be repeated.
- Stand facing the child, holding both hands and bounce up and down together. Stop, pause and see if the child requests the action to be repeated. Better still try this with the child standing on a mini trampoline!

Tips for teaching

- Create soft cosy corners or dens for the child to snuggle into. Try to make them big enough for two!
- Wind up toys or remote control toys are great to chase after.
- Make the most of a wet day by getting wrapped up and running and chasing through the puddles.
- Rocking and rowing rhymes as well as jogging on the knee rhymes are great fun for early interaction play.

Using water play

Why is this skill important?

- Some children with autistic spectrum disorders are fascinated by water. They may enjoy the sight and sound of water running, fountains or light rippling across the surface of water. Others intensely dislike the sound of water running, the toilet being flushed or the feel of water on their skin. As always, the need is to really know the individual child.

- Water play can be used to teach early interaction and communication skills, simple pretend play, and so much more.

- Self help skills need to be taught in a structured step-by-step approach, with consistent routines and real rewards. Getting ready for water play and drying hands after are idea opportunities to build self-help skills.

Water play and the EYFS Guidance

Children will probably be working at an early developmental stage such as:

- PD: move spontaneously within the available space; can stop; move freely with pleasure and confidence; combine and repeat a range of movements; use increasing control over an object by touching, pushing, patting, pouring

- CLL: use isolated words and phrases and/or gestures to communicate with those well known to them; use action, sometimes with limited talk that is largely concerned with the here and now

Ideas and activities to try

- Try water play in lots of different containers, different places, different colours, temperatures and so on.

- Try large marbles, shiny paper or foil, and bubble wrap bits in water.

- Use children's love of water play to teach simple pretend play routines, such as getting washed, bathing dolls, washing and drying dishes or clothes and so on.

- Use water play as a time to teach matching or selecting named objects.

- Play turn taking, pouring water through a water wheel or funnel.

- Try sending a wind up bath toy back and forth for some effective turn taking play.

- Take turns to drop suitable objects into water. Many children find the sight and sound satisfying. Try filling a metal tray or tin lid with water and dropping pebbles or similar objects for a rewarding clang and splash!

- Wash mitts make good water play puppets for 'Peek-a-boo' and 'Here I am' play.
- Try plant misters, hand held sprayers and toy water squirters for some turn taking fun.
- Try some rubber gloves and water filled balloons for tactile water play.

Tips for teaching

- Use a sand timer to limit the amount of time a child obsessed with water spends in the water. This can work well for those who love playing with running taps!
- Add water to small world play scenarios to entice children with autism to get involved.
- Encourage the child to explore by offering as wide a range of sensory experiences as possible involving water play.
- Use water play games to encourage the child to make choices, match and select objects, try out object use of everyday objects and use body language, gesture, pointing or words to make requests.

Using computers, television and DVDs

Why is this skill important?

- Most children with autism tend to have a visual learning style. They process information presented visually more easily than other information. Activities that present information visually include television, DVDs, cameras and computers.
- Children can control the volume and brightness of the TV and DVD image to make them acceptable. The repetitiveness of DVDs appeal to most children but particularly to children with autism.
- Computers present information consistently and visually. The information can remain on screen until the child has processed it.
- Computers, television and DVDs used carefully can help the child to absorb new concepts and relax.

Using ICT and the EYFS Guidance

Children will probably be working at an early developmental stage such as:

- CLL: use familiar words, often in isolation to identify what they do and do not want; use action, sometimes with limited talk that is largely concerned with the 'here and now
- KUW: show an interest in ICT; know how to operate simple equipment; complete a simple program on the computer, use ICT to perform simple functions

Ideas and activities to try

- Use short sessions with an appropriate DVD as a reward for completing other activities.

- Choose DVD that compliment themes included in the Foundation Stage curriculum.

- Scan photographs into the computer to make a photo album, visual diary or prompts for different activities.

- Use a digital camera to record sequences of simple pretend play, or perhaps different chunks of activity during the day. Breaking down complex sequences of activity into small chunks makes the information easier to process.

- Choose software that includes simple pictures of single objects, or teaches just one concept such as matching colours.

- Look for simple cause and effect programmes. You press the space bar and an action happens on the screen. Sit alongside the child and take turns to press the space bar.

- Try to build making choices and early interaction skills, such as anticipation and turn taking.

- Look out for simple nursery rhymes and songs on the computer. These present familiar information and words very visually and could be helpful.

   Give it a try. Every child is different!

Tips for teaching

- Choose videotapes and DVDs that are of educational value, are gentle, and use simple repetitive language.

- Some children may prefer to watch on fast forward! This is over stimulating and generally should be avoided, or at least limited by time, or perhaps restricted to just one DVD.

- Try and avoid computer software involving a child's special interests. This is likely to get in the way of their learning new concepts and skills.

- Use a definite end signal with the child – that is have a consistent routine that tells the child the time on the computer or with the DVD is almost finished, perhaps a song, and then covering the screen.

Using creative activities

Why is this skill important?

- Creative development poses particular difficulties for children with autistic spectrum disorders. They all have a rigidity of thinking that impairs their ability to be imaginative or creative, to represent one object with another, to explore and discover. The tendency is to aim for sameness and avoid change.

- Mark making has the potential to be hugely satisfying. It can offer the child a chance to release some emotions and commit some feelings and thoughts to paper.

- Simple pretend play, although limited in its creativity does offer the child some chance to learn through routines.

- Painting and messy play creative activities offer opportunities for early interaction.

- Some children may be particularly sensitive to certain sensory inputs, such as particular textures, smells, sights and sounds. The early years practitioner needs to be mindful of this when providing sensory play experiences.

Creative activities and the EYFS Guidance

Children will probably be working at an early developmental stage such as:

- CD: create and experiment with blocks, colours and marks; begin to combine movement, material or marks; explore colour and begin to differentiate between colours

- PD: use tools and materials for particular purpose; imitate and improvise actions they have observed

Ideas and activities to try

- Try finger painting with bubbly liquid on mirrors.

- Use a wide range of brushes with different handles, or sponge sticks to daub paint on textured paper and surfaces.

- Try painting with really drippy paint that can be dribbled from a height onto paper. Squeezing and dripping activities are difficult to resist.

- Play alongside the child with your own matching equipment, so that you do not invade their space.

- Encourage imitation. Start by imitating the child's spontaneous actions and then pause to see if they have noticed that you are copying them.

They may do a new action for you to follow, or perhaps you could try a new action for them to copy.

- Keep trying lots of different sensory play experiences. Try and work out why some are more appealing than others.
- Try some sensory play activities that do not involve getting hands messy – such as exploring different textures or sounds.
- Add some noise to the creative activity, perhaps trailing strings with tiny bells attached through different paint, or dropping plastic bricks dipped in paint onto paper or a metal tray.

Tips for teaching

- Think about the environment. Something as simple as the colour of the background paper, the feel of the brush handle or a breeze from an open window may be enough to put a child with autism off trying a new experience. Try to puzzle it out!
- Observe what motivates the child and try to use this to get them involved in creative play. For example, if the child loves sand play, try some sand art, or make a collage.
- Try giving the child plenty of space and freedom. Leave the materials out for some time. From time to time, go over and make some marks yourself but do not pressure the child into joining you. If they do give it a go, let them explore for some time on their own before trying to get involved.
- Make self-help a part of the activity but try not to let this become stressful to the child.

Using photos, pictures and books

Why is this skill important?

- Children with autistic spectrum disorders tend to process visual information more easily than information presented verbally, with all the social interaction this involves.
- Photographs of everyday objects and activities can be used as visual prompts or a visual diary or timetable. This helps develop understanding, reinforces routines and helps children know what is happening next.
- Pictures of objects may appear very different to the real object, or be symbolic of the real object. Children with autism tend to be very literal.

- The right book shared at the right moment offers great opportunity for shared attention, interaction and communication.
- Photos and individual pictures can be used in a step-by-step, structured approach to teaching communication and other skills. A match, select, name progression can prove helpful.

Using pictures and the EYFS Guidance

Children will probably be working at an early developmental stage such as:

- PSED: develop an understanding and awareness of themselves; seek out others to share experiences; make connections between different parts of their life experiences
- CLL: listen to favourite nursery rhymes, stories and song; join in with repeated refrains, anticipating key events and important phrases; use isolated words and phrases and/or gesture to communicate with those well known to them; enjoy rhyming and rhythmic activities; distinuish one sound from another; show an interest in illustrations and print in books, and print in the environment

Ideas and activities to try

- Give the child something to hold as you read – preferably an object related to the story.
- Give the child a mat or cushion to sit on, as a visual prompt.
- Try 'lift the flap' books. Play simple 'Ready steady go' games with the flaps to build anticipation.
- Make a photo album with just a few photos of people, places and objects of most significance to the child.
- Make looking at books part of a routine, with a fixed start and clear ending.
- Try matching real everyday objects to pictures in the book.
- Practise touch pointing to pictures of named objects and objects.
- If you find a book that works for the child, holds their attention and motivates them, look for books by the same author, or involving the same characters.
- Make your own books, or 'lift the flap' pictures, using photos of the child's favourite objects or characters.
- Make a simple posting box and play at posting named photos or pictures.

- Use photos and simple line drawings as visual prompts when asking the child to make a choice.
- Use cards from picture lotto and pairs games, to practice matching, selecting and naming everyday objects.
- Look for simple photograph board books of everyday objects. Use these for matching to everyday objects. Remember to make sure the child understands what the object is used for.

Tips for teaching

- Look for books with links to familiar characters or special interests, especially those with simple language and repetitive formats.
- Look for simple picture books about routines and events of particular significance to the child, such as babies, cars, homes and so on.
- Introduce new books slowly. Try to get the most from a few familiar favourites before introducing too many new titles.
- Try a wide variety of books, including books with a rhyming or repetitive text, giving the child plenty of repetition and anticipation key words or phrases. Photo books may be easier for them to understand.

Differentiation and reinforcement

Understanding differentiation

Throughout the Early Years Foundation Stage, each child will progress at their own pace and each child will have his own unique interests and learning styles. This is, of course, also true for children with autistic spectrum disorders. Generally, children with autism learn most effectively when activities are presented with visual clues and focus on their very specific learning needs. As many children with autism also have additional learning difficulties, the extent of their developmental delay will also dictate their individual learning needs. Like all young children they learn best from doing, from activities focused on everyday situations and routines of particular importance to them.

Children can be taught in different ways. This is known as differentiation. Differentiation ensures that teaching is most effective and the child makes the best possible progress.

Differentiation is a continuous process, changing in response to the changing needs of the child. It involves:

- recognising individual needs and learning styles

- ensuring planned activities are accessible and supplemented by additional support, so they are most effective in meeting the needs of the child

- observing, assessing and planning for each individual; precording and evaluating.

Differentiation can happen in the following ways:

Differentiation by the resources used
This could be using different toys, equipment or materials to make the activity accessible to the child, such as removing the distraction of a particular toy, or by using very simple clear photograph books.

Differentiation by the activity provided
This could be by providing a different but related task, such as matching pairs of everyday objects, instead of matching picture pairs, or a lotto picture game.

Differentiation by group size
This will depend upon the activity, and a child with an autistic spectrum disorder such as autistic spectrum may need one-to-one provision.

Differentiation by the way information is presented
Matching the way instructions and information are provided to the level of understanding, attention and listening skills and learning style of the child. It may also include using clues and prompts, perhaps real concrete objects or other visual prompts such as photographs.

Differentiation by the support provided
Matching the sort of support provided to the needs of the child at that moment. This may be a practitioner working alongside the child in a flexible and responsive way, to supply sensitive intervention or guidance as the child needs it.

Differentiation by the response or outcome expected
This could involve practitioners in expecting and recognising different responses from different children. The child with an ASD might make a pointing gesture rather than verbal response and they might only be able to listen for a short length of time on a particular activity.

Understanding reinforcement

The small step, structured approach, using prompts to support learning, provides plenty of opportunity to reinforce skill previously learnt.

Children need to have opportunity to:

- practise emerging skills often
- use these skills one-to-one and in small groups
- blend newly learnt skills with existing skills, such as having learnt to match pictures, the child needs to learn to take turns with another child (a previously learnt skill) to match the pictures, building towards playing a small lotto game
- to have time and opportunity to assimilate their learning and use it spontaneously, in different situations, with different people or independently.

Early years settings are ideally positioned for this, as there are plenty of chances to practice emerging skills as the settings provide:

- a wide range of different activities
- a flexible approach
- hands on learning
- different group sizes
- opportunity to use all the senses
- activities using everyday objects and routines.

When working with children with autism, considering differentiation and strategies for einforcing emerging skills is absolutely essential and will make all the difference to everyone involved.

and finally:

Early years practitioners can help develop children's skills by:

- modelling and teaching the child to copy actions
- using a structured small steps approach
- developing routines
- using prompts and clues
- making the most of physical play and music
- making rewards meaningful to the child
- focusing on play to teach communication and social interaction
- using obsessions and special interests as rewards for attention and achievement.

Who's who in multi-agency working?

Although many children with Autism in the Early Years Foundation Stage are likely to be still at the stage of assessment, concerns may well have been raised and a range of professionals will be available to offer the child and family support. This team will vary from place to place but is likely to include:

Speech and language therapist
Working often from a community health centre, specialist centre or from a child development centre at a hospital, speech and language therapists offer advice and therapy to build communication skills. Therapy may be direct one-to-one, or small group work, or maybe in the form of advice and support to parents, either individually or at a group.

Paediatrician
A hospital or community based children's doctor, often specialising in children with special needs.

Specialist pre-school teaching support or Portage worker
Specialist early years practitioners providing structured learning for babies and young children, often one-to-one in the child's home, and providing advice and support to parents.

Child development assessment centre staff
Either community or hospital based service providing specialist assessment, diagnosis and on-going support for babies and young children with special needs and their families

Educational psychologist
Responsible for offering advice and support to schools and for assessing the learning needs of children.

In addition there will be:
Social Services professionals
HomeStart volunteers
Occupational Therapists.

The team may also include parent partnership workers providing independent parental support. In addition, parents may receive advice and support from local or national voluntary organisations, such as local branches of the National Autistic Society.

Early years practitioners include:
setting managers
key workers
Special needs co-ordinator (SENCO)
who ensure the child has the best possible support from the team and an Individual Education or Learning Plan (IEP).

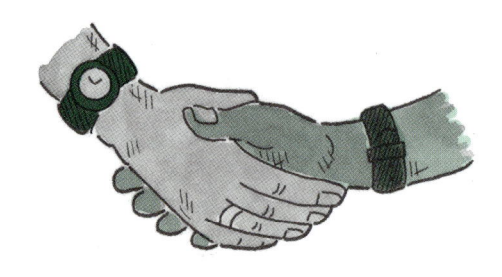

Partnership with parents

Page 14 will have given you some insight into what it might feel like to be the parent of a young child with autism. Establishing a good relationship with the parents will bring benefits to you and to them, and ultimately to the child. There is much you (and the parents too) can do to help establish a rapport:

- Make the time to listen to each other.
- Tune into their mood.
- Start and finish on a positive note.
- Ask their opinion.
- Try not to interrupt or say you know just how they feel.
- Let them know how much you enjoy working with their child.
- Find out what they want to know. Some parents particularly want to know what their child has had to eat or drink, what they have being doing, or who they are playing with. Ask them what they need to know.
- Get the message across that you see their child as an individual, not a child with autism.
- Mention what you have observed, such as 'I noticed that when I used the Thomas the Tank Engine book, he really concentrated well'.
- Give real positive messages, such as '*name* is really starting to respond to the use of bubbles to mark the end of activities'. Go on to describe the activity and be very specific in your feedback.
- Encourage them to bring in objects and photos from home. Where possible, let them take home particularly helpful resources to borrow, or visit the local toy library together.
- Take account of their priorities when setting targets.
- Work together on planning targets related to self-help skills.
- Be reassuring about meeting their child's toilet needs.

Early years practitioners can help all young children with autistic spectrum disorders by:
- being calm and focused;
- establishing routines;
- being consistent;
- being flexible and open to new ideas;
- always asking themselves 'why?';
- trying to see the world from where the child stands.

Early years practitioners can help parents by:
- making extra time to listen;
- attending multi-agency meetings;
- being positive;
- making the child's targets achievable;
- giving real and regular feedback about what their child has been doing;
- being sensitive to the parent's concerns about their child;
- giving a clear message that you like and respect their child as an individual, seeing them as a child first, a child with special needs second.

More ideas

- Put together a photo album of key objects, significant people and favourite toys and activities to share between home and your setting.
- Make a safe place for the child to put special toys or objects they need to bring from home. Make sure both parent and child know it will be safe, but accessible.
- Ask about the rest of the family, such as 'How is *name* with the baby?', or 'What does *name* like doing with his big sister?'
- Talk about what is happening to make inclusion work, such as practical examples of differentiation.
- Ask if you may observe a session when the speech and language therapist, or specialist pre-school teacher is working with the child, so that you can all make sure that you are working together most effectively.
- Make sure the parent has a copy of their child's Individual Education Plan and the targets across all areas of learning.
- If a parent is working or has little time available when they collect their child, do make other arrangements to meet informally to talk, discuss progress and listen to their concerns and aspirations for their child. A home–school diary sheet may help but is no substitute for getting together in person.

Different approaches to helping children with Autistic Spectrum Disorders

In this book, the focus has been on interactive play and a small steps structured approach to teaching new skills, differentiating the early years curriculum and providing opportunity to practice and reinforce emerging skills.

There are many different approaches to working with children with autism. These approaches, often suggested by parents or other professionals working with the child and family, vary widely.

Read on for a brief introduction to each approach and find out more about the programmes from the contact addresses on page 47.

SPELL

SPELL is an intervention pioneered by the National Autistic Society, proposing an approach based on the needs of the individual. The letters stand for:

Structure

Positive approaches and expectations

Empathy

Low arousal

Links

SPELL provides a framework for learning, the environment, organisation, training and much more. More details are available from the National Autistic Society.

PECS, Picture Exchange Communications System

What is it?

The Picture Exchange Communications System, first used in the United States, involves the child exchanging a picture of something they want for the actual item. It focuses on providing effective communication for children and in particular on the child initiating the exchange.

Early Bird approach

What is it?

This is a early intervention programme, developed by the National Autistic Society for children with autism and their parents. It is a three-month programme combining group training for parents with individual home visits, and includes video feedback of parents working with their child. The programme is based in South Yorkshire, but there are local programmes in many areas of the country.

TEACCH: Treatment and Education of Autistic and related Communication handicapped Children

What is it?

An American programme for the 'Treatment and Education of Autistic and related Communication handicapped Children'. This programme uses structured teaching and focuses on the physical environment in which children learn, the individual child's daily timetable, structure and organisation of each activity or task, and on the clues and prompts to help the child complete the task.

Options approach

What is it?

This is an intensive home based approach in which the parents and helpers first join the child in their autism and then encourage the child to find different activities and ways of relating. Developed in the US by the parent of a child with autism, this approach stresses the importance of the adults showing complete acceptance of the child and their actions.

Applied Behaviour Analysis, ABA or Lovaas programme

What is it?

Developed from the work of Dr Ivar Lovaas, this structured early intervention is a home based programme delivering up to 40 hours per week of intensive one to one teaching, using a structured small steps approach, with an exacting and sophisticated system of reinforcers and rewards.

Auditory integration training

What is it?

First developed to help children with hearing loss, this training is now used to help children with autistic spectrum disorders who have difficulty processing auditory information and who are hyper sensitive to certain frequencies of sound.

Resources and websites

For your bookshelf

SEN Code of Practice on the Identification and Assessment of Pupils with Special Educational Needs (DfES)

Thinking in Pictures
Temple Grandin

The Martian in the Playground
Clare Sainsbury

Including Children with Asperger's Syndrome
Sally Featherstone and Clare Beswick

Aspergers Syndrome - a Guide for Parents and Professionals
Tony Attwood

Also look at **www.earlysupport.org.uk**

On the Web

Any search engine will produce hundreds of results for autism. Start your search at the website of the National Autistic Society, at **www.nas.org.uk**. Also look at **www.earlysupport.org.uk**.

Also visit autism connect, **www.autismconnect.org** for a worldwide interactive personalised forum and notice board with latest information, research and training. For real insight look for personal accounts of living with autism. Try the work of Temple Grandin and Donna Williams, two very able individuals with autistic spectrum disorders who have written books and articles describing their very personal experiences of autism.

Search on **www.amazon.co.uk** for Asperger's syndrome - there are many guides, practical handbooks and individual autobiographies by individuals and their families. There are also lists of popular practitioner handbooks and story books for younger readers about children with autism.

Key Contacts

The National Autistic Society
393 City Road,
London EC1V 1NG
Tel: **020 7833 2299**

Autism help line:
Tel: **0870 600 85 85**
www.nas.org.uk

NAS EarlyBird Programme
3 Victoria Crescent
West Barnsley
South Yorkshire
S75 2AE

Tel: **01226 779218**
Email: **earlybird@nas.org.uk**

Peach (UK contact for ABA/Lovaas)
Parents for the Early intervention of Autism in CHildren
The Brackens,
London Rd,
Ascot,
Berkshire, SL5 8BE

Tel: **01344 882248**
www.peach.org.uk

Other titles in this series:

Working within the P Levels in the Foundation Stage — ISBN 9781408129517

Asperger's Syndrome in the Foundation Stage — ISBN 9781408129487

Attention and Behaviour Difficulties in the Foundation Stage — ISBN 9781408129531

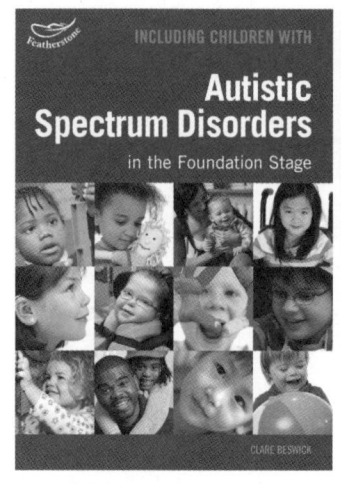

Autistic Spectrum Disorders in the Foundation Stage — ISBN 9781408129494

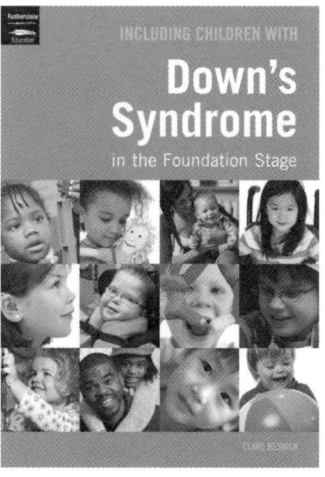

Cerebral Palsy in the Foundation Stage — ISBN 9781408129500

Dyspraxia in the Foundation Stage — ISBN 9781408129524

Down's Syndrome in the Foundation Stage — ISBN 9781408122648

Early Signs of Dyslexia in the Foundation Stage — ISBN 9781408120804

Working with Parents of children with additional needs — ISBN 9781408112533

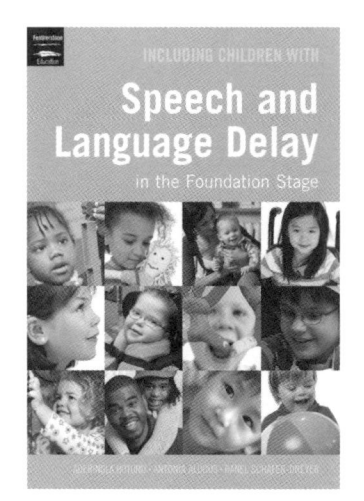

Speech and Language Delay in the Foundation Stage — ISBN 9781408114506

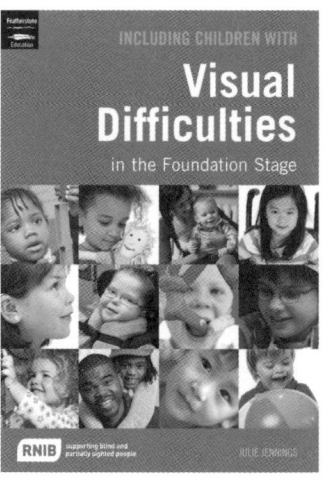

Visual Difficulties in the Foundation Stage — ISBN 9781408114490

All available from **www.acblack.com/featherstone**